19.95

The Library of the Civil Rights Movement™

Sit-Ins and Freedom Rides

The Power of Nonviolent Resistance

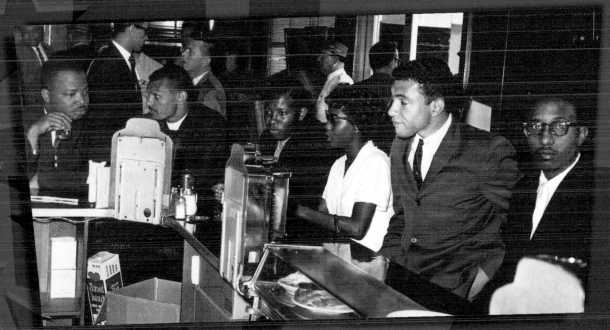

Jake Miller

The Rosen Publishing Group's

PowerKids Press™

New York

Published in 2004 by The Rosen Publishing Group, Inc.
29 East 21st Street, New York, NY 10010

First Edition

Editor: Frances E. Ruffin
Book Design: Emily Muschinske

Photo Credits: Cover and title page, pp. 6, 8, 11, 12 (inset), 13, 15 © AP/Wide World; pp. 5, 16, 19 © Bettmann/CORBIS; pp. 12, 20 © Lee Lockwood/TimePix; p. 19 (inset) © Paul Schutzer/TimePix; p. 22 © Donald Uhrbrock/TimePix.

Miller, Jake, 1969–
Sit-ins and freedom rides : the power of nonviolent resistance / by Jake Miller.— 1st ed.
    p. cm. — (The library of the civil rights movement)
Includes bibliographical references (p.) and index.
  ISBN 0-8239-6253-9 (library binding)
1. African Americans—Civil rights—History—20th century—Juvenile literature. 2. Civil rights movements—Southern States—History—20th century—Juvenile literature. 3. Southern States—Race relations—Juvenile literature. [1. Civil rights demonstrations. 2. African Americans—Civil rights. 3. Southern States—Race relations.] I. Title.
  E185.61 .M627 2003
                                                                                2001007243

Manufactured in the United States of America

Contents

Th Greensbo. o Sit-In

On February 1, 1960, four black freshmen from North Carolina Agriculture and Technical College sat down at the Woolworth's lunch counter in Greensboro, North Carolina. In those days most towns in America had five-and-dime stores, such as Woolworth's, where you could shop for school supplies, clothing, and household items. You could also get something to eat at their lunch counters. That day the four young men ordered only coffee, but they weren't served. Because of **Jim Crow laws** in southern U.S. states, black people were not allowed to eat at lunch counters or restaurants. They were supposed to place their orders off to the side, in another section of the restaurant. The food was put in a paper sack for them to eat somewhere else. Those four young men were tired of being treated differently from white people.

The first four sit-in protesters sat quietly at the counter in Greensboro, North Carolina, until the store closed, but they never got their coffee.

Then and Now

Sit-in protests became big news. The Greensboro sit-ins were among the first to get national attention from newspapers and television.

Young People Getting Involved

Lunch-counter sit-ins had been going on for a long time. There was one as early as 1942, in Chicago, Illinois. Many sit-ins were organized by the National Association for the Advancement of Colored People (**NAACP**), a **civil rights** group. College students and other young people tried to do their part to end **segregation**. Sit-ins were a way to end unfair treatment to blacks. They were tired of waiting for laws to be changed through court cases. Throughout the 1950s, adults such as the **lawyers** for the NAACP and the church organizers in Southern cities such as Montgomery, Alabama, and Little Rock, Arkansas, had won important victories. They had worked hard to end segregation in schools and on city buses. By the 1960s, Civil Rights became a cause for young people. Their **protests** had become big news around the world.

Even children in Oklahoma City protested against not being able to eat at lunch counters. They joined older students at lunch-counter sit-ins at a department store.

Protests Spread Quickly

After the first 4 students started the Greensboro sit-in, 27 students showed up at the lunch counter the next day. On February 3, 1960, protesters filled 63 of the 66 seats at the lunch counter. The protests quickly spread to colleges across the South. By the end of March, black students and some white students took part in sit-ins in 69 southern cities. New civil rights groups, such as the Student Nonviolent Coordinating Committee (SNCC), were founded to organize the sit-ins. Many whites in the South were against any form of **integration**, and they reacted violently to the peaceful sit-ins. They did not want blacks to sit at the lunch counters, so they attacked protesters at the sit-ins. Some even beat the protesters. The protesters were trained in **nonviolence**. They did their best not to respond to the attacks at all.

Some protesters were humiliated when mustard and sugar were poured in their hair. Often there were so many protesters, they had to sit outside the stores. The police arrested many protesters for disturbing the peace.

Sending a Message

In October 1960, Dr. Martin Luther King Jr., a famous civil rights **activist**, was arrested at a sit-in at a fancy department store in Atlanta, Georgia. Senator John F. Kennedy, who was running for president of the United States, promised to support the Civil Rights movement. Kennedy's brother Robert, a lawyer for the U.S. Department of Justice, arranged to get King out of jail. The protesters decided to send a message in a language that businessmen who ran stores like Woolworth's would understand. It was the language of money. Black people **boycotted** stores that refused to serve them or that did not hire blacks to work as salespeople. Sales at Woolworth's were lower than they had been the year before. The message got through. By July, businesses in Greensboro and in 27 other cities began to adopt some form of integration.

Dr. Martin Luther King Jr. is shown here after his release from jail. King had been arrested for participating in a sit-in protest at a department store in Atlanta.

The Freedom Riders

James Farmer founded the Congress of Racial Equality (CORE), a civil rights organization. He fought the Jim Crow laws in southern states that forced blacks to sit in the back of the long-distance buses. Blacks also had to use separate and less comfortable waiting rooms and restrooms at bus stations. In the spring of 1961, Farmer planned to lead a group of students, called Freedom Riders, on an integrated bus trip from Washington, D.C., to New Orleans, Louisiana. They would travel through several southern states where it was illegal for blacks and whites to sit together on the bus. Six whites and seven blacks, including Farmer, would make the trip on two buses, one Greyhound and one Trailways. Many people were afraid that the Freedom Riders would be attacked or even killed.

Dr. Martin Luther King Jr. meets with Freedom Riders. Inset: A bus driver is shown with a sign for a white waiting room. Inset this page: James Farmer founded CORE.

Trouble in Anniston, Alabama

The Freedom Riders met with several frightening and violent events on their trip south. On May 14, 1961, they rode into the small town of Anniston, Alabama. This is where they ran into their first real trouble. The first Freedom Rider bus was attacked by a mob of about 200 whites. The mob attacked the bus with clubs and chains and threw bricks through its windows. An Alabama state patrolman kept the mob from entering the bus. When the bus tried to leave town, it got a flat tire. The mob attacked again. This time someone threw a fire bomb onto the bus. When the nonviolent Freedom Riders climbed off the bus, they were viciously beaten. The Freedom Riders were turned away from the local hospital, because the doctors were afraid the mob would attack there, too.

This Freedom Rider bus went up in flames in Anniston, Alabama, when a fire bomb was tossed into a window.

Birmingham Police Fail to Protect Riders

The second Freedom Rider bus managed to avoid the mob in Anniston. Its riders made their way to Birmingham, Alabama, which was the next stop on their route. Everyone in Birmingham expected trouble when the bus arrived. Just before the Freedom Riders arrived, city police officers who had been at the bus station suddenly disappeared. Earlier, police had told the **Ku Klux Klan** that they could have 15 minutes alone with the Freedom Riders. When the bus arrived, an angry mob carrying baseball bats, pipes, and bicycle chains attacked. One Rider was hit in the head with a pipe and needed 53 stitches. Birmingham chief of police, known as "Bull" Connor, said the police were slow to respond to help the Freedom Riders at the bus station because they were home, celebrating Mother's Day. Connor had arranged for the police to stay away.

Freedom Riders who were beaten in a Birmingham bus station talked about the attack with a newspaper reporter.

The Freedom Rides Continue

After suffering two brutal battles, the original 13 riders took a plane to New Orleans. Another group of students from Nashville, Tennessee, arrived in Birmingham to take their place on the bus. Robert Kennedy had become U.S. **attorney general** when his brother John was elected president. To get the Freedom Riders out of Alabama safely, he had state police accompany them to the edge of Montgomery. Unfortunately, the local police offered them no protection. Once again the riders were brutally attacked by another mob. The mob didn't just attack the Freedom Riders. They lashed out at any black person whom they saw on the street. In the middle of the **violence**, the Montgomery police arrested the Freedom Riders for disturbing the peace. Rioters who attacked them were set free, even though the rioters were the ones who attacked and caused the trouble.

Freedom Rider Jim Zwerg recovers in a hospital from being beaten by an angry mob. Inset: *Freedom Riders Julia Aaron and David Dennis were protected by national guardsmen.*

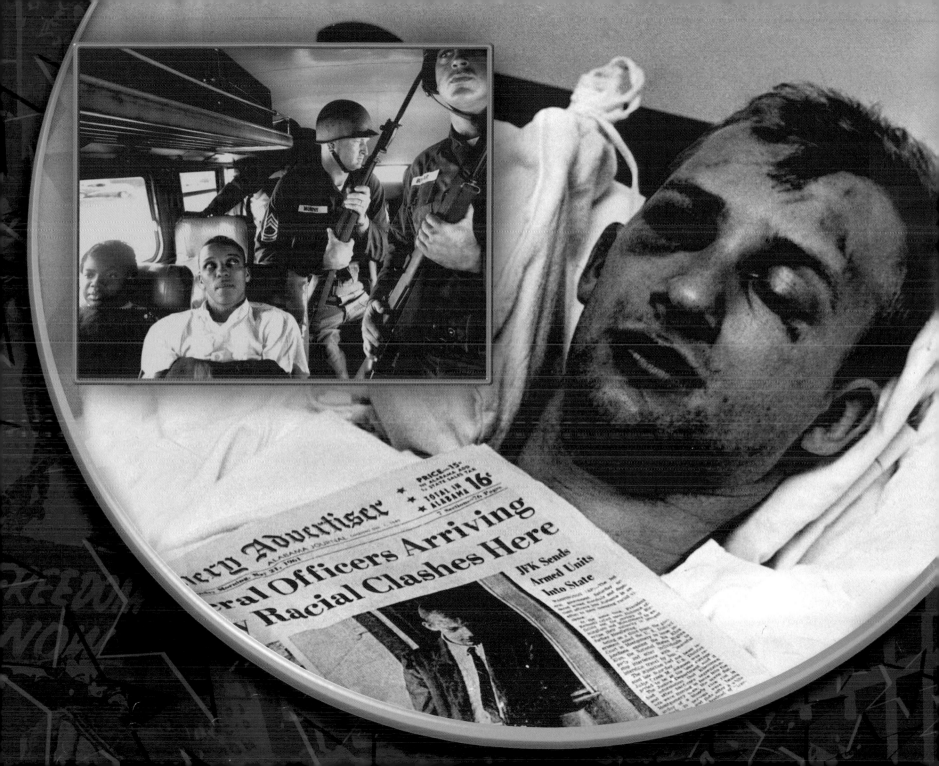

ery Advertiser
ALABAMA JOURNAL
*   *   *
PRICE—15¢
IN ALABAMA AND
U. STATE SALES TAX
TOTAL IN
ALABAMA 16¢
5 Sections—76 Pages

eral Officers Arriving

y Racial Clashes Here

JFK Sends
Armed Units
Into State

Violence and Arrests Did Not Stop Protests

President John F. Kennedy and his brother Robert made another deal with the officials in Alabama. They made a plan to let the Freedom Riders' bus continue to Mississippi with a police escort. The bus raced through the state at high speeds under heavy guard. When the bus reached Jackson, Mississippi, all the riders were arrested and sentenced to 60 days in jail. This was in spite of Kennedy's support for them. The whites who were against integration thought attacking the Riders and putting them in jail would put a stop to the protests. Instead, once the first busload made it to Jackson, Mississippi, another group of young people arrived to make the trip. They were religious leaders and students from around the country. They represented many civil rights organizations.

National guardsmen protect a Freedom Riders' bus. During the summer of 1961, Robert Kennedy and the courts worked to change unfair laws.

A New Generation of Heroes

The sit-ins and the Freedom Rides opened a new **era** in the history of the Civil Rights movement. For the first time, young people got involved to organize their own protests. They knowingly traveled to areas where they knew danger awaited them. They faced violence and arrest to demand fair treatment for all American citizens. Instead of using lawyers to fight unfair laws in court, they sacrificed their own bodies to show the world the horrors of **racism**. These young heroes were a great inspiration and example to generations of young people to come.

These Freedom Riders boarded a bus to travel through several southern states.

Glossary

activist (AK-tih-vist) A person who takes action for what he or she believes is right.

attorney general (uh-TUR-nee JEN-rul) Chief lawyer for the government, who helps the president to interpret and to enforce the laws.

boycotted (BOY-kaht-id) When a group of people refuse to buy a product or to use a service in order to bring about change.

civil rights (SIH-vul RYTS) The idea that all people can expect to be treated equally regardless of race, gender, or beliefs.

era (AIR-uh) A period of time or history.

integration (in-tuh-GRAY-shun) The act of bringing together groups from different races, genders, and social classes.

Jim Crow laws (JIM KROH LAWZ) Laws passed by southern states that kept people of different races separated in public.

Ku Klux Klan (KOO KLUKS KLAN) A white hate group.

lawyers (LOI-yerz) Experts who give advice about the law and who represent people in court.

NAACP National Association for the Advancement of Colored People. A group that fights for the rights of black people.

nonviolence (non-VY-uh-lens) A kind of protest in which the activists refuse to fight back against the attackers.

protests (PROH-tests) Events where activists demonstrate or speak out about issues.

racism (RAY-sih-zum) The belief that one group or race of people is better than another group of people.

segregation (seh-gruh-GAY-shun) The act of separating people of one race, gender, or social class from another.

violence (VY-lens) An act or acts of strong, rough force.

Index

Primary Sources

Cover: Black Freedom Riders have breakfast in the bus station in Montgomery, AL. It is the first time the eating facilities at the station are integrated. (1960). From AP/Wide World. **Page 5**: Four black college students sit-in in Greensboro, NC: Joseph McNeil, Franklin McCain, Billy Smith, and Clarence Henderson (1960). **Page 6**: Some of the 85 black children sitting-in at Brown's department store in Oklahoma City (1958). From AP/Wide World. **Page 8**: Whites pour food on protesters in Jackson, MS (1963). Photograph by Fred Blackwell. From AP/Wide World. **Page 11**: Dr. Martin Luther King Jr. following his arrest for a sit-in protest in Atlanta, GA (1960). From AP/Wide World. **Page 12**: Dr. King at a meeting with Freedom Riders. Photograph by Lee Lockwood. From TimePix. **Page 12 (inset)**: Mississippi Police Chief George H. Guy poses beside a segregation sign at the city's bus station (1961). From AP/Wide World. **Page 13**: Civil rights leader James Farmer. From AP/Wide World. **Page 15**: A Freedom Rider bus in flames (1961). From AP/Wide World. **Page 16**: Freedom Riders Jimmy McDonald and James Peck give reporters an interview after being beaten at the Birmingham bus station (1961). **Page 19**: Freedom Rider Jim Zwerg was hospitalized after being beaten (1961). **Page 19 (inset):** Freedom Riders Julie Aaron and David Dennis are protected by the Mississippi National Guard (1961). By Paul Schutzer. From TimePix. **Page 19 (inset): Page 20**: U.S. National Guardsmen surround a Freedom Riders' bus in Montgomery, AL (1961). By Lee Lockwood. From TimePix.

Web Sites

Due to the changing nature of internet links, PowerKids Press has developed an online list of Web sites related to the subject of this book. This site is updated regularly. Please use this link to access the list.

www.powerkidslinks.com/lcrm/sitinrid/